Introduction

The argument of gun ownership and the limits of the Second Amendment seem to infiltrate into just about any political debate these days. Such debates, along with elevating concerns of crime, terrorism, and general safety, have driven many citizens to purchase firearms.

There were guns in most homes during our nation's infancy and the presence of firearms remained in the majority of homes well into the twentieth century. But with more people migrating to urban areas, fewer folks hunted game, and as we progressed as a nation, well-trained law enforcement agencies were formed. These elements contributed to the decrease in the percentage of American homes with firearms. However, that is rapidly changing due to concerns of personal safety and family protection. More and more law abiding citizens are purchasing firearms.

With an increase in legal gun owners, there has also been an increase in firearms training and concealed weapon permits. As a firearms instructor, I have been posed with various questions pertaining to concealed carry. Quite frankly, there are no concrete answers for many of these questions, but I do want to address some of them in this short book. My purpose for compiling this information is to offer my clients, along with others, awareness that might be useful for concealed carry decisions. Some of the material in this book is routinely covered in a pistol safety course while some information might not be covered.

Neither this book nor its contents have been endorsed by any organization. It is simply a composition of information that I have acquired through training, experience, observation, and listening. My goal is not to bore you with statistics, but rather offer useful information and, in some cases, personal opinion.

Table of contents

Reasons to carry and should I carry?

Reasons for concealed carry are endless. Many choose concealed carry to fend off an assailant in the unfortunate event they are attacked. Some carry because their work requires travel into unsafe areas, and others may carry due to living in a high crime area. For me, it is about preserving our Second Amendment rights. As a high school social studies teacher, I am ever-mindful of how blessed we are to be protected by the Bill of Rights. My fear is that if we do not exercise our rights, we will lose them. Regardless, there are too many reasons that someone might choose to carry a concealed weapon to list them all.

There is no chronological standard for obtaining a concealed weapon license. Some citizens own a firearm but are not licensed for concealed carry while others may have a concealed weapon license, but own no firearm. It really doesn't matter if the license or the firearm comes first. Most firearm owners never even obtain a concealed carry license.

States vary in their concealed carry laws. Some states allow open carry while other states do not allow citizens to carry firearms at all. It is crucial to know your state's requirements. In Florida, a state with a population of more than 20 million, there are currently over 1.7 million citizens permitted to carry a concealed weapon.

To obtain a concealed weapon license in Florida, one must be at least 21 years of age and successfully demonstrate competency with a firearm. Applicants must also be a current resident and citizen of the United States or deemed a lawful permanent resident alien. Of course, those serving overseas in the United States Armed Forces are also eligible.

It is often a misconception that one must have a concealed weapon license in order to own a firearm, but that is not true. Again, many legal firearm owners never obtain a concealed weapon license. Their particular need for owning a firearm simply might not require concealed carry. Conversely, many people who do obtain a concealed weapon license actually never carry a firearm on their person. Not everyone, gun enthusiasts included, desires to routinely carry a firearm.

Of course, there are many reasons for concealed carry, and if you do choose to carry a firearm, it is imperative to have a concealed weapon license. Carrying a firearm on your person without a license could very well result in criminal charges.

Obtaining a concealed weapon permit is a personal decision that only the individual can make. There are a number of misconceptions concerning concealed weapon permits that I have heard, but found to not be true. For example, one individual asserted that obtaining a concealed weapon permit would require registering his firearm in a database. Another example is that individuals with a concealed weapon permit are bound by law to intervene in all critical situations. If the situation is so critical that an innocent person might die, most of us would certainly feel compelled to intervene whether we possess a license or not.

Sometimes, however, it is definitely a lose-lose situation to draw a weapon. Consider this situation: You are on a crowded sidewalk and suddenly observe someone being abducted directly across the street. Assume there are buildings behind the victim and his or her abductors, as well as traffic. If you pull a gun, the abductors might see you and begin shooting, risking the lives of those around you. If you shoot, the possibility exists that you will hit the victim or an innocent person inside one of the buildings. No one would be expected to draw a weapon in such a situation. Instead, quickly unholster a cell phone, call 911, get photos, and write down any description possible.

I realize this picture might seem rather "Hollywood" or unrealistic. But, here is the reality. Many situations that would warrant unholstering your weapon are not going to be ideal situations for discharging that firearm. Perhaps this is why some law enforcement officers oppose concealed carry. While I am a huge proponent of concealed carry, I do understand their argument. That is why we must be responsible when carrying concealed weapons.

Now, back to the argument in support of concealed carry. Certainly the reasons to obtain a concealed weapon license outweigh the reasons not to. Perhaps the one drawback to obtaining a license is the cost, which is only a little over $130 for seven years. That is less than $20 per year. Of course, there is the one-time cost of a pistol safety course for those who need it. The cost of the course runs anywhere from free to around $120. It is advisable to take a pistol safety course even if you are experienced with handguns.

Handling safety and various techniques are introduced, taught, and reviewed. Firearm safety courses are a great resource for useful information and safe practices for firearms enthusiasts of all levels. As an instructor, I am constantly learning.

Choosing a firearm

One of the most frequent questions that I hear is, "Which gun should I buy?" Well, like ice cream, there are many available options to choose from. Again, this is a decision that must be made by the individual who will carry and own the firearm. There are many things to consider when buying a firearm for concealed carry, with cost and availability of ammunition being among the concerns. Reliability, comfort, and stopping power are at the top of my list. Ease of maintenance, capacity, and accuracy are also rather important.

Unfortunately, gun owners usually have to compromise one or more options or features they deem important in order to get what they want in a gun. A friend who owns a local gun shop once told me that most gun owners, especially men, continue their search for the "holy grail" of guns. He stated that they will endlessly buy and trade guns in search of that perfect carry.

Some, like myself, will have a primary carry weapon but own other guns for various reasons. My personal choice for a daily carry is the Glock 43, a sub-compact 9 mm. The most common complaint that I hear about the Glock 43 is that the factory magazines only hold six rounds. Of course, there are aftermarket magazines that will increase your capacity by a couple of rounds. However, that still isn't suitable for many gun enthusiasts.

Some gun owners prefer a revolver, usually a double action, while most today prefer a semi-automatic. I personally prefer firing revolvers on the range, but find many advantages to carrying semi-automatics. The first advantage is the ease of concealment. Even semi-automatics with a low ammo capacity, such as the Glock 43 or LCP .380, match the round capacity of a revolver and the ease and speed of changing magazines exceeds that of reloading a revolver, even when using speed loaders. Having said that, I realize there are many gun owners who are extremely quick in reloading a revolver and can feasibly reload quicker than me, even when I am using a semi-automatic.

Many gun owners who conceal carry often have two or more guns on their person. Their backup gun can often be found in an ankle holster. Of course, there are those who carry revolvers or derringers that are capable of shooting .45 Colt Ammunition or .410 shotgun shells. These are especially popular among farmers and timber workers because of snakes and other dangerous creatures.

We haven't even gotten into long-barrel guns. My first choice for home defense is my trusted Remington 870, a .12 gage pump shotgun. Of course, that is a personal choice and many will argue why they might choose another weapon for home defense. As one can easily see, the choices are endless. Again, the right gun depends on the individual, his or her lifestyle, size, physical condition, and preferences.

When selecting a firearm, spend time on the internet conducting research. It's fun visiting different sites, looking at prices, reading reviews, and comparing options. Perhaps the most important thing to do is visit a local gun shop. You will find the proprietors are most helpful and willing to answer questions. Generally, they are extremely knowledgeable and will gladly answer your questions. It is important to gather as much information as possible about firearms and properly using them.

While chain stores frequently offer exceptional prices on certain items, local gun shops are usually competitive in their pricing and are unsurpassed in service beyond the sale. The local gun shop is a great place to learn about the firearm you intend to buy.

A client recently asked if I would recommend buying a used firearm, and without hesitation, my response was yes. However, I advised him to purchase from a local gun shop. Purchasing firearms from individuals can lead to problems, especially if the gun was stolen or used during the commission of a crime. We must remember that buying a used firearm, especially from a gun shop is much different than buying a used automobile or lawn mower. In many cases, the gun has been used very little and well-maintained. In some cases, the previous owner was simply a gun enthusiast in search of that "holy grail" of guns.

Again, I would look for reliability first. If it fails to eject casings on the range, it will likely fail to eject when you need it most. I certainly wouldn't want to have a health insurance policy that may or may not

19

pay when I need it, nor would I want a daily carry that may or may not shoot when my life depends upon it. Comfort is crucial when carrying a concealed weapon. If it is too bulky, it will become too easy not to carry.

While stopping power is paramount in concealed carry, I would be hesitant to tell someone to carry nothing less than a .357 Magnum. They might choose to carry nothing at all and a .22 caliber single action revolver still beats a pocket full of rocks. An entire book could be written on stopping power because so much comes into play. First, there is the mental state and condition of the aggressor. The location of the bullet's penetration and possible organs hit should also be factored in.

Fortunately, I have never shot a human target and pray that I never do. However, I am aware that it would be much more difficult to shoot with the marksmanship that I do when firing at a still target for pleasure. Of course, the ammunition you use will have a bearing on stopping power as well. Be sure to discuss the appropriate ammo with your gun salesman.

Before you carry

Once you find your "holy grail" of guns, or at least your first step toward that "holy grail," it is time to become familiar with the firearm. Learn to disassemble, clean, and reassemble it. Purchase some dummy rounds to practice loading and unloading. If your local gun shop doesn't stock them, they can easily be found online.

Learn the ballistics of the ammunition that your gun will shoot and determine the brand and type of ammunition that you need. Most gun enthusiasts keep range ammo in addition to the ammo kept in their firearms for protection. Again, an entire book could be written on this subject so I will humbly advise you to discuss the ammo needed with the gun shop staff. It is imperative that you communicate your needs.

As I mentioned earlier, read online reviews about the firearm that you have purchased. You can usually obtain answers to questions you have or any malfunctions you may experience.

Carry method

Many firearms are indeed expensive, but concealed carry gear and clothing can be too. Autumn and winter offer many options for carrying concealed weapons, but spring and summer present quite a challenge for weapon concealment. Concealment is the goal, unless you are in a state that allows open carry. It is not only a goal, but it is required by law in most states. Unfortunately, concealed weapon license holders can and do experience trouble for failing to properly conceal their weapon.

One example is that of a tow truck driver. Because his work often led him from home late at night, the gentleman made the decision and obtained a concealed weapon license. During a call late one night, he laid on his back to hook a disabled vehicle when a young, conscientious state trooper noticed his shirt had ridden up, exposing a holstered firearm. From all accounts, the scene was pretty ugly for a while, but the trooper eventually took the situation into consideration, returned the weapon to the truck driver, and allowed him to go about his business.

During cooler weather, I find it extremely easy to carry a concealed weapon. I usually wear a vest or coat with an inside pocket and can easily conceal my handgun. In fact, some of my coats are just long enough that I can carry in a belt holster and still be adequately concealed. The last thing that I want, however, is to take a stroll through the mall and hear a child yell, "Mommy, mommy, that man has a gun!"

Just to be on the safe side, I almost always carry my weapon concealed inside a garment. Many people are fans of the inside the waistband holsters. I will not criticize them, but wearing an inside the waistband holster simply isn't for me. Perhaps they would be more appealing if I would lose a few dozen pounds. Many people rely on an ankle holster for concealing a backup weapon and some use ankle holsters as a primary method of concealment.

One of the most comfortable approaches of concealment that I have found is the holster shirt. It is simply a tee shirt with a built in holster. For the fashion conscious, the colors are limited to pretty much black and white. I own a cotton holster shirt and will soon purchase more. The one drawback is the delay posed in unbuttoning one or two outer shirt buttons to retrieve the firearm. Of course, a snap button shirt or light windbreaker in lieu of a button up shirt will easily solve that problem.

A couple of other methods that I am compelled to mention are concealment purses for ladies, and concealment cases that resemble a cell phone case. Such cases are designed for compact and subcompact handguns and are available through the website sneakypete.com.

Regardless which method you choose, just remember the goal is concealment. Can you imagine going home from the late shift, stopping at a convenience store for a gallon of milk, and the new clerk on duty sees the grip of your Glock and panics as you reach up for the milk on the top shelf? It is essential to take the extra steps necessary so no one else knows you're carrying a firearm.

Here is another scenario to consider. You're going home from the late shift and stop at the same convenience store where the clerk knows you well. You're propped up against the counter, sipping a cup of coffee that he or she just brewed. A stranger enters the store, heads back to the milk case and notices the grip of your Glock protruding from inside the waist of your trousers. You're listening to the woes of the clerk and fail to notice the stranger, who happens to be a robber, is quickly approaching with his own weapon drawn.

You are now a prime target without a chance.

It really doesn't matter which concealed carry method you choose, as long as it keeps your firearm concealed and you are comfortable with it. Just remember, your life, along with the privilege of legally carrying a concealed weapon could depend upon it.

Should I keep a round chambered?

Perhaps one of the most difficult questions posed is whether or not to keep a round chambered in a semi-automatic pistol. Well, a double action revolver that is loaded only requires pulling the trigger to fire a round. How is a semi-automatic different? Still, many people are skeptical of carrying a round in the chamber even with the gun holstered.

Again, this is a personal choice. Perhaps you've seen the video portraying an assailant with a knife attacking a female victim. Time does not allow her to chamber a round before the simulation reveals that she would likely sustain mortal wounds. The other version of the simulation shows the woman carrying a semi-automatic pistol with a round chambered, having just enough time to get off a few shots and avoiding mortal wounds. Nonetheless, she would likely receive wounds in that scenario as well.

Perhaps the best advice that I've seen pertaining to the question of keeping a round chambered was posted somewhere online. Simply leave your semi-automatic empty and cock it. Carry the weapon as you might normally carry it for a few days and see if the trigger has been pulled at any point. Just don't forget to treat it as if it is loaded. Always treat an empty gun as if it is loaded. My grandmother often said that people are killed more often with empty guns than with loaded guns.

Carrying sensibly

In most cases, citizens with concealed weapon permits are required by law to carry weapons in a concealed manner. While many people argue for the right to carry in an open manner, I would still prefer to carry my firearm in a concealed manner. First, it alleviates any undue suspicions that others might have when they see my firearm. Also, some folks, even staunch conservatives and proponents of the Second Amendment, have an existing fear of guns that will never be erased. I personally would be neither happy nor comfortable if I walked into a restaurant and several patrons were sitting around with snakes wrapped around their arms. I suppose we all have our fears.

Another reason that I would prefer to carry my weapon in a concealed manner is because of the risk of having it taken away by a deranged individual, criminal, or even a terrorist. Finally, I prefer to appear to pose little or no threat if placed into a situation that I must use my firearm to defend myself or someone else. I learned many years ago in defensive tactics training that the elements of speed, skill, and surprise are essential in prevailing over an opponent. Speed and skill comes through repetitive practice and training. One way the element of surprise can come is through appearing to have no weapon.

With the right to carry a weapon comes the role of responsibility. We must be responsible with our firearms and carry them sensibly. A concealed weapon permit is not a license to seek out trouble or brandish our firearm. It certainly does not make us bulletproof, an expert, or invincible.

Unfortunately, there are those who might fantasize about performing a heroic act. There are others who give into the temptation of "showing off" their weapon. With that being said, a very low percentage of citizens licensed to carry concealed weapons commit crimes using their firearms, misuse their firearms, or act irresponsibly. Some research, as limited as it is, indicates that number is even below one percent.

In short, most gun owners are responsible citizens and gun owners who possess a concealed weapon permit are even more likely to exercise responsibility due to training and awareness. Education seems to breed more education and knowledge. Furthermore, we do not want to lose our privilege of concealed carry. Nonetheless, when a crime is committed by a concealed weapon license holder, the media will certainly let it be known the individual was licensed to carry a concealed weapon. As a result, our Second Amendment rights are further attacked and threatened. Always remember, the liberal media do not want us to carry guns.

The issuance of a concealed weapon permit should remain confidential and not advertised. In other words, obtaining a license to carry is nothing to be ashamed of, but it shouldn't be bragged about either.

Certainly we should not be compelled to engage in a blazing gun battle or seek to join the ranks of Doc Holliday or Wyatt Earp. Instead, we should make every effort to avoid being thrust into the media's spotlight, giving leftwing politicians and activists ammunition to further diminish our right to bear arms.

A wise, elderly lady once told a newly elected official that any fool can be seen on the evening news, but it takes an astute individual to avoid media attention. The same holds true for gun owners. There are simple steps to avoid trouble and media attention. First, we should constantly be observant of our surroundings. We should also be cautious of where we go and where we carry our firearms.

Being observant of our surroundings should be the norm whether we carry a concealed weapon or not. It's just plain common sense. It should be practiced at home, work, church, while shopping, at the movies, or wherever we go. Recent events have taught us that the criminal element and terrorists do not discriminate their targets.

Look for suspicious vehicles, individuals, or packages. Are your pets acting strangely? Be observant of busted doors and windows. Are doors and windows closed when they should be open or open when they should be closed? Are lights off that should be on or on that should be off? Do friends, neighbors, or relatives act distraught or distracted? If you strongly suspect that something is not right, quickly call upon local law enforcement. It is always best to err on the side of safety.

Another way to sensibly and responsibly carry a concealed weapon and avoid trouble is to be cautious of where you go. When carrying a firearm, it is wise to avoid places and areas that are prone to trouble. It is not advisable to take that evening walk or jog through a section of town known for robberies, drugs, and violence just because you're "packing heat." Unfortunately, too many people carry weapons with a false sense of security. Chances are, if someone legally carrying a concealed weapon becomes engaged in a confrontational situation, he or she might never get the opportunity to draw their weapon. Remaining observant and avoiding areas susceptible to trouble will, however, decrease the odds of being victimized. Parties and gatherings noted for alcohol, drugs, and rowdiness should always be avoided, especially when carrying a firearm.

When entrusted to carry a concealed weapon, we must be ever-mindful of when and where we carry that weapon. While carrying a concealed weapon should be comfortable and almost second nature, we should be conscious of the fact that firearms aren't allowed everywhere, even with a concealed weapon permit. It is imperative to know where concealed carry is allowed in your state or any state that you visit. It is also vital to learn if other states you visit are reciprocity states. Do they recognize your concealed weapon permit and if so, what are their concealed carry requirements? You never want to travel away on vacation and return home on probation. According to the Florida Department of Agriculture and Consumer Services, carrying a concealed weapon is prohibited in the following venues in the State of Florida.

- Any place of nuisance, such as a known gathering spot for criminal activity.
- Any place where the carrying of firearms is prohibited by federal law
- Area technical centers
- College or university facilities
- Courthouses and courtrooms
- Detention facilities, prisons, or jails
- Elementary or secondary school facilities
- Inside the passenger terminal and sterile area of any airport

- Legislative and legislative committee meetings
- Meetings of the governing bodies of a county, public school district, municipality, or special district
- Police, sheriff, or highway patrol stations
- Polling places
- Portions of an establishment licensed to dispense alcoholic beverages for consumption
- School administration buildings
- School, college, or professional athletic events that are not related to firearms

Some of these venues may have exceptions or additional restrictions and this information may be verified and updated by visiting the FDACS website at freshfromflorida.com. It is wise for concealed weapon license holders to periodically check the restrictions in their state as laws and policies do change.

Knowingly and willfully violating any provision set forth by Florida Statute constitutes a misdemeanor of the second degree and that person is subject to charges. Needless to say, carrying a concealed weapon has its boundaries and limits.

Many years ago while training for a job in the pest control industry, I had many questions of my mentor concerning various scenarios and situations. Finally, he told me, "When in doubt, don't." Throughout my career with the Florida Department of Corrections, and now education, I have considered those words of wisdom countless times. When in doubt, don't. These words certainly apply to concealed carry. If your intuition tells you that you probably shouldn't be carrying your weapon, you probably shouldn't be carrying your weapon.

Various offices or businesses prohibit firearms on their premises. In some cases, their policy is understandable and in some cases the policy is not so understandable. Many will argue the case that statute clearly states where firearms cannot be carried and they will not relinquish their weapon. Once again, I would personally prefer not to bring any undue attention to myself. In this case, I will always choose to simply and voluntarily comply with the wishes of management and business owners.

One example that I heard was of an individual who was suspected of carrying a concealed weapon. Although he had a legal permit to carry the weapon, he was asked to secure the firearm in his vehicle. When he refused, he was asked to leave the premises. Had he not left at that point he could have been charged with not only trespassing, but trespassing with a firearm.

The purpose of including this information is to neither ignite a debate nor frighten anyone who legally carries a concealed weapon. Instead, it is to reiterate how quickly emotions and differences of opinion can cost gun owners the right to carry a concealed weapon.

While I will not deny that gun owners with a concealed weapon license should not be so restricted in the places we are allowed to carry a firearm, I would much rather be allowed to eat half the cake instead of none of the cake.

Lawfully carrying a concealed weapon also requires responsibility, sensibility, and respect when interacting with law enforcement. We must never forget that we are still private, law-abiding citizens. Members of the law enforcement community are the ones charged with the responsibility of protecting the public. While I concede that there are a number of law enforcement officials who are not necessarily proponents of private citizens being permitted to carry concealed weapons, I maintain and truly believe that most law enforcement officers are not opposed to it.

In the event someone is stopped by a law enforcement officer for a traffic violation, or anything for that matter, it is highly recommended to inform the officer that they are carrying a concealed weapon by permit. I have heard officers from various departments comment that this is no issue for them and they do appreciate being informed.

Always remember, law enforcement is here to protect and serve the citizens. In their presence, I will gladly allow them to do so. If time and opportunity allows in their absence, I will contact law enforcement to fulfil their duty and give them ample opportunity to do so.

Law enforcement deserves our unabashed support and appreciation. They often have a thankless job and, like in most professions, have a split second to make decisions with critics spending days, weeks, and even months scrutinizing such decisions. Having said that, I have always and will always support law enforcement.

A concealed weapon permit does not constitute me being a free-lance cop. First and foremost, I am not trained as a law enforcement officer. Assuming I encounter a law enforcement officer attempting to catch a suspect and decide to assume the role of a Good Samaritan in coming to his or her aid, the officer might mistake me for an accomplice of the suspect, which could result in my arrest.

At best, the law enforcement officer would realize that I was simply trying to help, but would then be burdened with the responsibility of my well-being. Simply put,

I would likely be in the way and instead of aiding law enforcement, I may very well be aiding the suspect. In summary, if an officer is found in a problematic situation, he or she shouldn't have to face the burdens of distraction and protecting someone else. We can often best serve as a witness, obtaining detailed description.

Conversely, if a law enforcement officer is being attacked and his or her life is in danger, I have no doubt that he or she would gladly accept the help of a Good Samaritan. It is doubtless that any law-abiding citizen would then be happy to fulfill the role of a Good Samaritan in that situation.

Should law enforcement need assistance from private citizens, they will certainly request that assistance. Though I have rarely seen such a call for help, I have seen it nonetheless.

Unfortunately, law enforcement cannot be everywhere and that, along with exercising our Second Amendment rights, is why we carry concealed weapons. In the unfortunate event that we are forced to use a firearm in self-defense or in the defense of another, it is paramount that we are in compliance with the law. Again, review your state laws regarding concealed carry and know your state laws regarding the use of force and the use of deadly force.

Florida Statutes, Chapter 776 defines justifiable force, deadly and non-deadly. It is important to know that according to F.S. 776.012, a person is justified in **using** or

threatening to use **deadly** force if he or she reasonably believes that using or threatening to use such force is necessary to prevent imminent death or great bodily harm to himself or herself or another or to prevent the imminent commission of a forcible felony. A person who uses or threatens to use deadly force in accordance with this subsection does not have a duty to retreat and has the right to stand his or her ground if the person using or threatening to use the deadly force is not engaged in a criminal activity and is in a place where he or she has a right to be, according to the text of F.S. 776.012.

This is where things get tricky. In recent months, I have heard two very reputable gentlemen from my community at separate times state that they wouldn't want to carry a firearm to shoot someone. Instead, they would rather use it in a threatening manner to halt or defuse any potential assault or harmful act. According to Florida Statute, there is a justification in threatening the use of deadly force. However, a simple argument with the threat of deadly force and presentation of a firearm could very well result in criminal charges.

Simply presenting a firearm as leverage in an argument is a costly decision. Relying on a firearm should always, always be the last means of survival or protection. In the event one is forced to discharge his or her firearm, firing that weapon should cease once the imminent threat has subsided. Carrying sensibly is indeed a good insurance policy to have, but like all insurance policies, we pray that we never need it.

Never present a weapon unless there is reasonable belief that deadly force is necessary to prevent imminent death or great bodily harm to yourself or another person or to prevent the imminent commission of a forcible felony. Florida Statute defines forcible felony as treason; murder; manslaughter; sexual battery; carjacking; home-invasion robbery; robbery; burglary; arson; kidnapping; aggravated assault; aggravated battery; aggravated stalking; aircraft piracy; unlawful throwing, placing, or discharging of a destructive device or bomb; and any other felony which involves the use or threat of physical force or violence against any individual.

Based on the State of Florida's definition of a forcible felony, deadly force certainly wouldn't be justified in all forcible felonies. For example, if I discovered my neighbor attempting to burn his home with no one inside, I would not be justified in shooting him. Yet, arson is among the crimes listed as a forcible felony. However, if my neighbor was attempting to burn his home with bound hostages inside, I would be justified in using deadly force.

Again, with the privilege of carrying a concealed weapon comes the role of responsibility. That responsibility is coupled with accountability and in the event that deadly force is used, we, like law enforcement officers, have a split second to make a decision with critics spending days, weeks, and even months scrutinizing that decision.

Along with responsibility and accountability, there are many safety measures to adhere to when carrying a firearm, most of which are covered in basic pistol safety courses. Along with observing the safety practices taught in basic pistol safety courses, I must emphasize these seven thoughts.

1. Avoid escalating situations
2. Know your surroundings
3. Never shoot into a crowd.
4. If you or the one you are protecting stands a better chance of living without presenting a firearm, do not unholster.
5. Relying on a firearm should always, always be the last means of survival or protection.

6. In the unfortunate event you are justified and forced to present your firearm as a legal means of survival, be prepared and willing to shoot. If not, the criminal will likely use **your** gun to do harm to you and possibly others.
7. In the event one is forced to discharge his or her firearm, firing that weapon should cease once the imminent threat has subsided.

Conclusion

If concealed carry is for you, enjoy the opportunity and stay abreast of current laws, firearms, ammunition, and accessories. Become involved in competition shooting, even if it is merely friendly competition with a friend or relative. Safely using firearms can prove to be an enjoyable sport that is challenging and engaging. Like any other hobby or sport, it can become very expensive. However, there are some inexpensive firearms out there of suitable quality to enjoy at the range.

There are public and private firing ranges available for your enjoyment. Visit them, learn from other gun owners, and make new friends. Those fortunate enough to live in a rural area with a couple of acres or more can easily set up a personal range with very little investment. In fact, a safe, suitable range can be established for less money than most firearms cost.

Go out and target practice often and always practice the safety procedures learned in your pistol safety course. No practice will ever simulate a real life situation in which a firearm might be used, but even marginal practice will better prepare us for such an ill-fated confrontation than the preparation that no practice at all might provide. Practice on the range will assuredly improve your familiarity with the firearms that you own.

I pray that you never have the need to use any firearm in a survival situation. However, a firearm, opposed to a concrete mixer or printing press, is one of those tools that you would rather have and not need than need and not have.

Practice safety daily, target practice often, and enjoy your "holy grail" of firearms always.

About the Author

In addition to being a teacher of United States History and Government, Jeffry Boatright is a firearms instructor and an avid supporter of Second Amendment rights. In short, he believes in our Constitution, appreciates the freedom that we enjoy as Americans, and recognizes that freedom hasn't been free.

After spending the majority of his career as a state correctional officer, Jeffry ventured into the field of education. As a firearms instructor, the North Florida native incorporates his passions for firearms, safety, awareness, teaching, and people.

www.ingramcontent.com/pod-product-compliance
Lightning Source LLC
Chambersburg PA
CBHW060647290526
45793CB00001B/436